Writers'

Colors

and

Dreams

~Ophelia – Marie Flowers

To Geni Butterfield – May you always see
the simple things – like dew drops, and sun-
beams and new spring leaves – as beautiful. May
you see the colors and marvel.
     God bless,

          ~Ophelia-Marie Flowers

A very special thanks goes to *Alex Mintah*
for all her in-depth help with this book
over several months – critiquing, answering
questions, giving suggestions, and all around being
a joy.
Thank you so much.

ISBN-13: 978-1500871055

ISBN-10:1500871052

This book is dedicated to Shawnie E. Kirkwood
who is forever delighting and inspiring me
with the colors, shapes, depth, and true emotion
captured in her writing.

You play with strands of woven glass
and weave story flecks
of essence
in such a beautiful way –
When I read your words,
I long to see the world
a little more like you do.

wovenglass.wordpress.com

You Within The Story

12/7/13 Age: 18

Show me now
A story clearly written.
Show me how
The words were brought life.
Show me now
The lives were simply tokens
Of a world that you make broken
To match the one you're in.

Show me how
You wrote yourself inside there.
Show me now
The pieces of your soul.
Show me how
You write within the pages
A heart locked up in cages
And yet you've set it free.

Show me now
The heartbreak of your story.
Show me how
It breaks the hero's stand.
Show me now
The hero lost and falling
With none to hear the calling –
But we know that's not the end.

Show me how
The hero finds the strength.
Show me now
The hope that flickers on.
Show me how
They fought to win their freedom,
Ran away and built the kingdom,
That lives inside your dreams.

Show me how
Life changed for the better.
Show me now
What the readers never saw.
Show me how
The story keeps on growing,
And everything worth knowing
Are whispers of your heart.

Show me now
Where you find the wonder.
Show me how
You write to share your dream.
Show me now
The love you have for writing
And the fires are worth lighting
For the truths you brought to light.

Show me now
The reason you are writing.
Show me how
You let the colors flow.
Show me now
All you wish that I was seeing
And the things that change the meaning
Of the writer's heart in you.

Show me how
You live within your writing.
Show me now
The questions you have raised.
Show me how
Things are worth believing,
And the impact you are leaving
Is why you choose to write.

Dragon's Life

5/22/10 Age: 15

Flame of anger, slash of claws.
Dragon's life that holds no laws.
Step of warrior, blade of skill.
Dragon's life – not easy kill.
Voice of thunder, eyes of blue.
Dragon's life from me to you.
Dance of freedom, spinning fast.
Dragon's life for me to last.
Laugh of joy, movement bold.
Dragon's life with heart of gold.

Nature Dance

10/4/13 Age: 18

Fire dance,
Let the heat drain away the chill –
Drink in the warmth and laugh.
Will you allow anyone
To take the roaring light
From your grasp?
Hold it tightly,
Though it burns.
Crackle! Spark! Glow!
Now it whispers,
Now it rushes,
Now it fades and sways in glowing embers.
"Fire dance
And never die."

Rain dance,
Let the droplets strike your skin –
Lift your hands and twirl round.
Will you allow anyone
To take you from this wild call?
Face the thunder,
Though it roars.
Patter! Strike! Shout!
Now it soaks,
Now it floods,
Now it churns and bursts in misty rainbows.
"Rain dance
And never cease."

Sky dance,
Let the wind stretch around you –
Watch the prairie grass sway.
Will you allow anyone
To bind your feet to the ground again?
Clutch the whirlwind
Though it screams.
Blow! Whistle! Cry!
Now it presses,
Now it spins,
Now it swirls and slides through every crack.
"Sky dance
And never fade."

Never die.
Never cease.
Never fade.
Never, ever stop the dance –
The edge
Drops out of sight
Where the fires die,
The rains cease,
And the winds fade to a bare whisper...
Don't fall over that edge.
Dance, dance, dance and dream about tomorrows,
Though the fire burns,
Though the thunder roars,
Though the whirlwind screams –
Don't lose hope.

Will you echo the song?
The song of fearsome bravery
Of fiercely tangled dreams?
Will you continue the dance?
The dance that's laughing
Deep in your soul,
Crying out in every pounding rhythm?
See the wild beauty –
Don't let the light be taken,
Don't let them steal you from the call,
Don't touch the ground with bound feet,
Never to rise again.
Crackle. Glow. Spark.
Patter. Strike. Shout.
Blow. Whistle. Cry.
And dance –
Never forget to dance.

Music's Dance

9/26/13 Age: 18

Dance around, let the music patter.
Feel the rain falling down, down, down.
Move, dear friend, let the rhythm steal you,
Past the thoughts hiding in your frown.

Dive beneath, let the music ripple.
Feel the waves lapping near, near, near.
Swim, dear friend, let the current reach you,
Strike down deep to the sound so clear.

Smile alone, let the music whisper.
Feel the sun shining bright, bright, bright.
Run, dear friend, let the warmth release you,
Leap and twirl through the dawn's first light.

Sing again, let the music shimmer.
Feel the wind blowing 'round, 'round, 'round.
Laugh, dear friend, let the music take you
To the dreams drifting toward the ground.

Shout aloud, let the music gather.
Feel the sound growing strong, strong, strong.
Sway, dear friend, let the music fill you,
Hold the joy finding you belong.

Just believe, let the music shatter.
Feel the shards as they sting, sting, sting.
Live, dear friend, let the music pierce you
In your heart where your voice takes wing.

Look inside, let the music wander.
Feel the tune twisting out, out, out.
Reach, dear friend, let the music stretch you
Past the coils in your sea of doubt.

Splash within, let the music color.
Feel the song rising high, high, high.
Sit, dear friend, let the music touch you
Deep inside where your heart now flies.

Creature

5/26/10 Age: 15

The roaring of a creature I had never met.
The roaring of a creature that makes me tremble yet.
The soaring of a creature that I have never touched.
The soaring of a creature
While down below I hunched.
The landing of a creature
With loudest thud of all.
The landing of a creature
That leaves a frightened awe.
The beauty of a creature I ne'er before had seen.
The beauty of a creature with scales in vibrant sheen.
The laughter of a creature I had never known.
The laughter of a creature
With eyes that brightly shone.
The smile of this creature
With giant dagger teeth.
The smile of this creature, but still there's no relief.
The touch of this creature; as gentle as a breeze.
The touch of this creature makes my body freeze.
The voice of this creature is a rumble low.
The voice of this creature says he's friend not foe.
This huge and hulking dragon
Gives me a tiny grin,
Then soars into the sky; a dancer of the wind.

Waiting To Be Wakened

6/7/14 Age: 19

I'm just a moment
Waiting to be wakened.
It's a story
And it's shaking
To the core
Of all I know.

Did I see it
When it listened
With heart songs drifting
Through the cracks
And flowing
Between each faded wall?
Oh it was magic
Born of laughter
And hemmed through
With silver flecks.
All the colors
Drifted inward
Until we breathed
Every moonbeam into our chests.
And we laughed amid it all
Because it sang
Our very souls into joyful
Harmony.
'Twas both powerful
And yet so gentle
When we glided through the beats

That hummed beneath our skin
Like so many stories
We'd forgotten...

Tell me
Did you hear the stars playing
On the night they started to fall,
Or did you simply
Twirl away
As always?
Did you slide down the crescent moon
To the edge of twilight
And whisper in the still air?
Maybe you did
And if so
I wish I had come along to dance with you...
It would have been glorious
To watch you gliding along
With the falling stars singing mournfully
As a backdrop.
To have watched it all fade
Might have wakened me again
To see the melodious teardrops
Hanging in the creeper vines
That spiral up the oldest trees.
Tasting their strength
As if it were their own...
Who knows what stories I could have seen
If the drifting steps had taken me
On a different course.

But for now I won't dwell on that.
I'm just a moment waiting to be wakened
With a story shaking me
To the core of all I know.

Driven To The Ocean

4/10/14 Age: 19

We were
Nine upon the shoreline
And we were
Calling to the sea.
We were
Tugging at the moor lines
As we were
Longing to be free.

We were
Motion's last emotion
And we were
Standing on the edge.
We were
Pining for the ocean
When we were
Dancing on the ledge.

We were
Lights lit so delightful
And we were
Singing to the stars.
We were
Powerful and frightful
But we were
Covering the scars.

We were
Great that was unrated
And we were
Plunging in the waves.
We were
More than understated
And we were
Meant as no man's slaves.

We were
Best yet still untested
And we were
Ready then to rise.
We were
More than was requested
But we were
Aiming for the skies.

We were
Want that proved unwanted
And we were
Called to plunge below.
We were
Never cowed or daunted
No, we were
Ripples forming slow.

We were
Found and yet unfounded
And we were
Laughing to the deep.
We were
Motion yet ungrounded
But we were
Certain what to keep.

We were
Wet, lit by the sunset
And we were
Finally at the source.
We were
Said to be a no–threat
But we were
Held by Ocean's force.

Silver Flecks Falling

8/23/14 Age: 19

Butterflies floating
On a midnight range.
Colors of morning
In the midst of change.
Silver flecks falling –
Do you find that strange?
I don't.

Melodies floating
In a wordless daze.
Dew drops of morning,
In a twilight haze.
Sliver ice falling –
Will you chase this craze?
I will.

Happily floating
With a radiant grace.
Brightness of morning
As I lift my face.
Silent rain falling –
Do you know this place?
I do.

Fairies

9/28/14 Age: 19

Pull the windows open,
Let in the wayward breeze.
Laugh at all the fairies
Drifting through the trees.

The colors of tomorrow,
Send ripples through today,
Melodies of yesterdays
Bring laughter as they play.

Dreaming

10/24/14 Age: 19

Tell me, Dreamer,
Do you hunger for the lightning
To burst upon you as clarity
To see beyond the shadow-fog?
Do you feel the frigid fingers
Probing at your mind
With insistent harmonies?
Will the stillness shift around you
Until it deafens the murmured hum
That echoes beneath your skin?
Tell me, Dreamer,
Do you find yourself flickering
With words you can't remember,
Yet they tickle at your memory?
Are there stories you recall
As soon as they prance at the boundaries
Of your sleepy rest
But are driven away
In the morning's light?
Ah, Dreamer,
I would show you how the pieces twine
If I could only find the threads' end.
The cold is seeping
Through the edges of my mind.
Crystal patterns catch the light
And ricochet in rainbows
Across my face.
I am left

Drenched with wispy glimpses
Of hues I can almost remember
But the dreams keep trailing
To barely grace my fingertips.
I rest
With wind-sung moonbeams
Casting silver silhouettes
Down the staircase
I can't remember
Carving –
Singing of tomorrows
When I'll capture the fragments
And find how the cracked reflections
Show slivers of my soul.

I've Got Music

7/10/14 Age: 19

I've got music in my heart –
Pounds out deeply,
Quivers, starts.
Oh, the words just fall apart
Now.

I've got music in my mind –
Trembles weakly,
First-steps, blind.
Oh, the notes we leave behind
Now.

I've got music in my soul –
Whispers sweetly,
Heartfelt, whole.
Oh, I feel I've found my goal
Now.

I've got music in my chest –
Colors steeply,
Never rests.
Oh, I've finally passed the test
Now.

I've got music in my voice –
Echoes meekly,
Quiet choice.
Oh, the reasons we rejoice
Now.

Forgotten Whispered Wind

8/10/13 Age: 18

The dark of this night is only broken
By a slice of moon
And a smattering of cloud-shielded stars.
Chilled northern wind whispers
Through the bleak mountains
And swirls
Through the gathered mist.
Silence flows in steady ribbons
With nothing but the wind's rustle
To interrupt.

Shhh. Be still.

The stars begin to fade
And the sky shifts from black
To the gray of growing light.
Shadows cast their long fingers in looming shapes,
Clinging to the dark,
But daybreak's glow
Steadily grows.

Silence breaks
With the first trilling whistle of a bird.
Dawn's colors dance on the horizon,
Casting warm tendrils
Over the cold stones.

Ah, smile, dear one. Here comes the morning.

Music's Threads

5/1/14 Age: 19

The words
Keep swirling –
Light,
And dark,
And full of memories.
I dance among them
Knowing both the pain
And the joy
Of the music's whispers.
The current
Is speckled
With dappled lights
And I can't
Bear to pull myself away.
It's a melody,
Woven in,
Pulling out,
Twisting through again
As the memories surge inside.
Do you hear it
Thrumming in my chest?
Threatening to burst free?
Ah,
Powerful harmonies
Weave deep scars
Across my heart
With colored threads
And blackened wire –

Faster,
Closer,
Knitted tight –
I twirl in the unraveling mess
With laughter pouring through my skin
To shatter all the mirrors
That reflect only lies.
They seek to crush me as they fall
But I dodge the glass shards
My footsteps bounding circles
Past those fears.
I am music
And
Motion
Whirling through the glass
My threads fraying
And wires twisting
Down my arms,
While the music pulses inside me.
Music,
Threads,
Wire,
Glass,
And me
Dancing through it all;
My heartbeat on the edge
Of the memories.

Dragon Song

9/13/10 Age: 15

If you only listen,
I'm sure you would hear,
A sound that would bring you
Both wonder and fear.
A dragon is singing
A heart-rending song,
Of days when his kind
Were revered and strong.
They would dance on the wind
And scream of their power,
But now they appear only
To sing in night hours.
They used to be colors
Of red, gold, and green,
But now they are grey –
They have lost their fine sheen.
The dragons are hidden
To all but a few,
But I bet if you'd listen,
You'd hear their song too.

Alive With Joy

4/13/14 Age: 19

Oh we laughed
'Cause we knew
Life was a moment.
But we were
So
Alive
With Joy
That it couldn't matter
For we had found
True delight.

Oh we dreamed
'Cause we knew
Life was a moment.
But we were
So
Alight
With hope
That things would get better
And we would
Fly again.

Storm

8/2/14 Age: 19

The clouds shiver with droplets
Ready to release.
Thunder trembles bass
While lightning laughs
Along the edges
In sudden scrawling tendrils.
With a shuddering of wind
The droplets plunge from the clouds
To splat on the cracked ground
And seep away.
Dry plants raise their leaves
With longing to the skies
As the water droplets fall
To ease their thirst once again.

Mountain View

1/25/15 Age: 20

In the mountains
Dipped in snow
As the cold drifts
Pile below –
As the North winds
Dance and blow,
Hear the music,
Whisper slow.

With the echoes
In the cold
As the mountains
Tremble, old –
As the bobcat
Stalks out, bold,
Watch the sunset,
Tinged with gold.

Touch The Heartcry

9/12/14 Age: 19

There's a story murmuring
On the edge
Of my mind's drifting
Silver ponderings...
But
I can only grasp
The first words,
"Touch the heartcry."

So I gather wisps of longing
Bound
In those simple words
And try to weave them
Deeper
To find their meaning.
Ever on the tip of my tongue –
Balancing on my fingertips –
Those words laugh at my attempts
To meld them
Together.

"Touch the heartcry."
Find your freedom
In delving
Within
The echoes of wonder.
Brush the lighter strokes
With shaded fables
Of long ago
Memories.

Press away
Shadow drifts
Clouding out the longing cries.
Distractions of the moment
Bid the heartcry
Stay silent in its zeal to be
Heard.
So sell the nightmares
Into bondage –
Never listen
While the ripples dance spirals
Across your mind
And wind deeper in worries
We should forget –
Never bow to the calling
That would drive you
Away.

There's a story murmuring
On the edge
Of my mind's drifting

Silver ponderings...
But
I can only grasp
The first words,
"Touch the heartcry."

So I hold it
With all I am...
For some day
I shall claim the next words
And find the story
Waiting for me
Beyond tomorrow.

In That Moment

12/20/14 Age: 19

There were a thousand stories
In that moment,
And you gathered them up
In wild delight,
Your pen dancing over the paper,
And smudging ink,
As if the words might fly away
If given the chance.

You seemed to have found
The simplest of truths
And yet, the way you wrote it
Burst upon my mind
Like glinting stardust –
Reminding me of the hope
Singing just beneath the surface
Of the memories.

There was an almost childlike wonder
In the way you scribbled down
Each delicate fragment,
Each complicated phrase –
Binding them together
With experience
And imagination.
Only you could see
With your writer's eyes...
In that moment.

Moonlit Daydreams

8/17/14 Age: 19

Silver dreams of solitude,
Spinning shafts of light,
Dancing through the tree boughs,
Whispering in the night.

Solid turns of attitude,
Singing in their might,
Tossing back the nightmares,
Taking back the fight.

Shapeless hopes of fortitude,
Shimmering in my sight.
Memories mixed with daydreams,
Finding wings of flight.

Silent joys of gratitude
Shivering with delight,
Laughing at the wonders,
Bathed in moonlit white.

Writer's Droplets

8/19/14 Age: 19

Splash the written worries
Trailing
From your fingertips –
Puddling
And slipping
Into the cracks of your mind.
Draining trickles
Find life amid the pages
Of a wrinkled notebook.
Scrawled with inky lines –
Swirled into arching letters
Of a writer's pen.
It is almost calming,
To have the emotions flow from within
And find release
In little pools of words –
Bold rivulets of longing,
Tempered with droplets of memories,
All running together
As melded stories
Mixed with dreams.

Whatever Calls Inside You

1/15/14 Age: 19

Take the pain and make it music,
Take the tears and make it song;
Write the colors of the rainbow
Into worlds where we belong.

Take your fears and fill the canvas,
Take your doubts and fill the page;
Write your worries down upon it
As it ripples from each stage.

Take the ache and make it stories,
Take the hurt and make it light;
Write the things you can't remember,
Though they haunt you every night.

Take your cries and fill the darkness,
Take your dread and fill the miles;
Write the words beneath the surface
Of our weariness and trials.

Take the dark and make it shudder,
Take the black and make it real;
Write the hope that keeps you going
Through the terrors that you feel.

Take your past and fill the future,
Take your steps and fill the road;
Write to show the path you're walking –
Where you've been to lift that load.

Take the noise and make it silence,
Take the bound and make it free;
Write the heart behind your smiles
Where you're hiding broken pleas.

Take your loss and fill the empty,
Take your grief and fill the void;
Write in sorrow steeped with candor
Not as something to avoid.

Take the year and make it moments,
Take the day and make it flow;
Write whatever calls inside you;
Write a story most don't know.

Take your dreams and fill the oceans,
Take your hopes and fill the skies;
Write to tell the world new days
Where they need not feed the lies.

Take the joy and make it color,
Take the hope and make it sing;
Write the life that finds belonging
In the words that others bring.

Take your life and fill the weary,
Take your faith and fill the weak;
Write the grace that God has given
And the truth we long to seek.

About The Author

I'm a homeschool graduate and full-time certified nurse aide who does a little writing on the side. ;) I enjoy reading long Fantasy books, hanging out with my friends, teasing conversations, and living this life to the best of my abilities for God.

If you'd like to contact me, you may email me at ophelia-writer@hotmail.com

Or visit my blogs:

za-blogging.blogspot.com
&
in-which-i-talk.blogspot.com

I would love to hear from you!

~Ophelia — Marie Flowers
Zeal Aspiring

ZAFE

Made in the USA
Middletown, DE
22 February 2015